PLAYLAND

PLAYLAND
Athol Fugard

faber and faber
LONDON · BOSTON

First published in South Africa in 1992 by Witwatersrand University Press
This edition first published in Great Britain in 1993 by Faber and Faber Limited
3 Queen Square London WC1N 3AU

Photoset by Parker Typesetting Service, Leicester
Printed by Cox & Wyman, Reading, Berkshire

A CIP record for this book
is available from the British Library

ISBN 0-571-17058-7

2 4 6 8 10 9 7 5 3 1

For Yvonne Bryceland

Playland was first performed on 16 July 1992 at the Market Theatre, Johannesburg, presented by Mannie Manim Productions, with the following cast:

MARTINUS ZOELOE	John Kani
GIDEON LE ROUX	Sean Taylo
'BARKING BARNEY' BARKHUIZEN (Voice off)	Bill Flynn

Director	Athol Fugard
Designer/Assistant director	Susan Hilferty
Lighting	Mannie Manim
Sound	Mark Malherbe
Production manager	Wesley France
Stage manager	Melanie Dobbs
Deputy stage manager/sound operator	Christo Boshoff
Deputy stage manager	Haccius Mokopakgos
Wardrobe	Hazel Maree
Production assistant	Debbie Falb

Playland was first performed in England at the Donmar Warehouse, London, on 25 February 1993, with the following cast:

MARTINUS ZOELOE   John Kani
GIDEON LE ROUX   Sean Taylor
'BARKING BARNEY' (Voice off)   Bill Flynn

Associate Director and Designer   Susan Hilferty
Sound Designer   Mark Malherbe
Lighting Designer   Mannie Manim
Tour Manager   Wesley France

*A small travelling amusement park encamped on the outskirts of a
Karoo town. A large sign with the name PLAYLAND is prominently
positioned. There is also an array of other gaudy signs advertising the
various sideshows and rides – the Big Wheel, the Wall of Death, the
Ghost Train and so on. They are all festooned with coloured lights
which will be switched on when the night gets under way. Battered
speakers of a PA system at the top of a pole.*

*Foreground: the night-watchman's camp. A broken car from one of
the rides with a square of canvas stretched over it to provide shelter
from sun and rain, and a paraffin tin brazier.*

Time: the late afternoon of New Year's Eve, 1989.

GIDEON LE ROUX *saunters on. Casually but neatly dressed for a
warm Karoo evening. He is stopped by the sound of an angry voice
with laughter and heckling from other voices.* MARTINUS ZOELOE
*walks on from the opposite side. Old overalls, and a rolled-up
balaclava on his head.*

MARTINUS: Ja! Ja! Go on. Laugh as much as you like but I say it
again: I'll see all of you down there in Hell. That's right. All
of you. In Hell! And when you wake up and see the big fires
and start crying and saying you sorry and asking forgiveness,
then it's me who is laughing.

(GIDEON *stands quietly smoking a cigarette and listening to the
harangue.* MARTINUS *is not aware of his presence.*)

MARTINUS: Ja! That day it is Martinus who has a good laugh.
You tell lies and cheat and drink and make trouble with the
little girls and you think God doesn't know? He knows! He
sees everything you do and when the Big Day of Judging
comes he will say to you, and you, and specially *you*: Hey!
You fucked the little girls in Cradock and gave them babies;
you fucked the little girls in Noupoort and gave them babies
– what you got to say for yourself? And you got nothing to
say because it's true and that's the end of it. And all the times
you verneuk the baas with the tickets and put the money in
your pockets, he knows about that as well. And also the

I

generator petrol you are stealing and selling in the location. Baas Barney swear at me, but I know it's you. I see you there by the petrol drums when you think nobody is looking. So voetsek to all of you!

(*He sees the white man for the first time.*)

GIDEON: (*Applauding*) That's it my friend. That's what I like to hear. Somebody who is not afraid to speak his mind. So you tell them. You tell them loud and clear.

MARTINUS: Joburg skollies. All of them. All they know is to make trouble for other people.

GIDEON: Then go make some for them. Ja. Report them to your baas. Don't let them get away with it. You got to speak up in this bloody world. It's the only way to put an end to all the nonsense that is going on. Everywhere you look – bloody nonsense! People think they can get away with anything these days. There's no respect left for nothing no more.

MARTINUS: That one with the skeel oog, he's the one. The first time I see him there in Beaufort West, when he comes looking for work, I knew! Skelm! And I warn Baas Barney. That one is trouble I tell him. But he wouldn't listen. So now we have it.

GIDEON: Then to hell with your Baas Barney as well! That's what I say. If he won't listen then too bad. You tried your best. My advice to you is just carry on and do your job and to hell with everything else. What is your job here?

MARTINUS: Watchman and handyman.

GIDEON: Night-watchman for Playland. That sounds okay.

MARTINUS: Night and day watchman.

GIDEON: All the time?

MARTINUS: All the time. I watch everything all the time.

GIDEON: So when do you sleep?

MARTINUS: I don't sleep.

(*A silence settles between the two men.* GIDEON *tries again.*)

GIDEON: Bloody hot again today, hey? On the news they said it was thirty-six degrees in the shade here by us. In the shade, mark you! (*Hollow laugh.*) I like that. I felt like phoning them and asking, is that now supposed to be a joke or what? Over by De Aar it was forty-one. Can you imagine? Chickens

2

was dying of heat stroke. De Aar! (*Shakes his head.*) God knows this dump is bad enough, but De Aar! No man, that's a fate worse than death. They say there's a ou bollie there who fries his breakfast eggs on his motorcar bonnet in summer. Says he uses multi-grade instead of margarine. (*Hollow laugh. No response from* MARTINUS.) Anyway that's how bad it is. Couple of months ago they offered me a transfer there with a pay rise. I turned it down flat. (*Pause.*) By the way, what's your name?

MARTINUS: Martinus.

GIDEON: Martinus. That's a good one.

MARTINUS: Martinus Zoeloe.

GIDEON: That's sommer a bakgat name, man! Martinus Zoeloe. B G. Buitengewoon. So listen, Martinus, when do things get going around here? You know, the lights and the music and everything. When do you people switch on?

MARTINUS: Seven o'clock.

GIDEON: (*Looking at his watch*) Hour to go, then five more and it's hip-hip-hooray time hey! Goodbye 1989, welcome 1990! And 'bout bloody time too. Hell, this year now really went slowly, hey? I thought we'd never get here. Some days at work it was so bad I use to think my watch had stopped. I check the time and I see it's ten o'clock. Two hours later I check it again and it's only half-past ten.

(*Hollow laugh. Nothing from* MARTINUS.) Didn't look as if it was going to be so bad in the beginning. I got my discharge at the end of February and it looked as if things were going to be okay – you know, being home, being alive . . . (*Hollow laugh.*) . . . and everything. I mean, shit man, there I was waking up in my own bed again with my old Ma bringing me a cup of condensed milk coffee the way I use to dream about it up there on the Border. Ja, March was also all right. I had some good times. Even April. But then . . .! Shit-a-brick! June, July, August, September – fucking nothing, man! All of them. Just nothing. And I tried. Believe me I tried, but I just couldn't get things going again. Every day I wake up and say to myself, 'Come on now Gid, get your arse in gear and let's get things going today' . . . but that's as far as it gets.

3

Like my pigeons. I use to be crazy about pigeons. Me and my Dad. Just before he died we had over a hundred of them in a hok there in the backyard. Tumblers, Pouters, Homers, Racers, Fantails – we had them all. This was the time they use to flock – you know, all come together and fly around before settling into the hok for the night. Hell that was a beautiful sight, man. Aerial monoeuvres of the Karoo Squadron we use to call it. All the time in formation, round and round in the sky!

You would think they was following orders the way all them would suddenly swerve and change direction . . . (*He laughs at the memory.*)

Then after my Dad died . . . I don't know . . . somehow it just wasn't the same any more without him. I kept them going and all that – fed them and cleaned the hok – but my heart wasn't in it the way it use to be when he was also there. Then one morning I go to feed them and – *Here!* – a wild cat or something had got into the hok in the night and gone mad! Half of them were lying around in pieces, man – dead as fucking freedom fighters . . . I had to pull the necks of another ten of them that was still alive they was in such a bad way. That did it. I sold the rest of them and I thought that was the end of it. Not a damn! I'm sitting up there on the Border one day – and this is now years later, remember – and I suddenly find myself thinking about them and how lekker it would be to start up again – buy a few breeding pairs, fix up the hok and watch them fly at sunset. From then on that was all I use to think about. You got to have something to think about up there man, otherwise you go mad. I'm not joking. I've seen it happen. Anyway, the truth of the matter is I haven't done a bloody thing about it since I've been back. The old hok is still standing there on three legs, ready to fall over, full of spider webs. I don't know what it is, man, but I just can't get things going again. I'm not bosbefok or anything like that. The doctors have given me some pills for my nerves and to help me sleep, but otherwise I'm okay. Ai! It's just . . . I don't know. Like tonight. I was ready to just sit at home with my Ma and fall asleep in front of the

4

television again. Can you believe it? New Year's Eve? That's when I thought to myself, 'No man, this has now gone far enough. Get out Gideon le Roux. Get among the people. Join in. Grab some fun. Look for romance!' So here I am ladies! Don't all rush at once. (*Hollow laugh.*)

Anyway . . . that is going to be my resolution tonight when midnight comes: No bloody miseries next year! I don't care how I do it, but 1990 is going to be different. Even if it kills me, I'm going to get things going again.

You got yours ready?

MARTINUS: What?

GIDEON: Your New Year's resolution.

MARTINUS: What is that?

GIDEON: Midnight, man. When 1990 comes. You give up smoking or something like that.

MARTINUS: I don't smoke.

GIDEON: Then something else. Drinking.

MARTINUS: I don't drink.

GIDEON: Well there must be something you want to give up.

MARTINUS: No.

GIDEON: Okay. So you're perfect. Good luck to you. (*A hip flask of cane spirit appears out of a pocket.*) That means I don't have to offer you a dop hey! (*Hollow laugh.*)

Last year I gave up drinking. It lasted about ten minutes because then I needed a drink to give up smoking, and then I needed a drink *and* a cigarette to give up wanking – and that's not the capital of China, my friend! And so it went. Every dop was another resolution . . . that lasted ten minutes! Base Camp Oshakati! That was quite a party. Talk about your friends going to Hell – if you had seen me and my buddies that night you would have sent the lot of us there as well.

(*Another silence. Both men stare at the horizon where a Karoo sunset is flaring to a dramatic climax.*)

How about that, hey!

MARTINUS: Ja, it's starting now.

GIDEON: It might have been a useless bloody year, but it's certainly going out in style. I mean, look at it! It's right around us. That's sommer a cinerama sunset for you.

MARTINUS: Ja, it's going to be a big one tonight.

GIDEON: We use to get them like that up in South West. From one end of the sky to the other – red, red. I'm telling you man, it looked like the end of the world had come. And believe me there was a couple of times when it also felt like that.

MARTINUS: The Day of Judgement.

GIDEON: That's a good one. I like it. Days of Judgement! Ja, for a lot of men that's what they turned out to be. And they were good men. My buddies! But that's the way it was. One day you're swapping jokes with him, the next day you're saying prayers for him . . . and wondering if it's your turn next. (*Pause.*)

I can remember sitting there in the bush one day. It was about this time – late, late afternoon, nearly getting dark. That sky wasn't just red my friend, it was on fire! And you could smell it too. Smoke, burning rubber, ammo, dust, bush . . . everything! We'd had a big contact with SWAPO that day, and we weren't expecting it. They caught us napping. Jesus it was rough. Anyway, it was klaarstaan time again – sunset, sunrise, SWAPO's favourite times for a hit – and one of my buddies comes and parks next to me there in the trench. I say to him, 'We're alive, Charlie. We're alive.' And Charlie says, 'You know Gid, I'm not so sure any more that that's the good news.' I always remember that. Because he was right. It always only got worse.

MARTINUS: (*Gesturing at the sunset*) I watch it every night. Every time it is different and I see different things.

GIDEON: Free bioscope!

MARTINUS: Last night it was like gold.

GIDEON: I didn't see it last night.

MARTINUS: (*Pointing*) That way, on the road to Beaufort West. Big, big piles of the gold that makes them all mad in Johannesburg. Mountains of gold!

GIDEON: How about that hey? Mountains of gold! We'd all be millionaires.

MARTINUS: And then sometimes nothing happens. The sun goes

6

down slowly, slowly, and then it's gone. And then the light goes away slowly, slowly, and then it's also gone, and it's dark and the stars are shining.

GIDEON: They say it's just the dust in the atmosphere what does it. You know . . . the colours and the clouds and everything. But even so it still makes you think, doesn't it? Like over there, that big one. Doesn't it look like they finally dropped the atomic bomb on De Aar? I mean look at it. That's the atomic bomb cloud. What do they call it again? Ja, the mushroom cloud!

MARTINUS: Tonight I see the fires of Eternal Damnation.

GIDEON: Hell, that's a heavy one.

MARTINUS: That's right, Hell!

GIDEON: Well, I suppose if you believe in that Bible stuff it could be, but speaking for myself . . . (*shakes his head*) . . . no thank you. I had the Bible shoved down my throat since I was small and I'm gat-full of it now man. I've got a bad dose of religious indigestion.

MARTINUS: Hell Fires on the Day of Judgement!

GIDEON: Don't get yourself all excited my friend, I've told you, it's just dust in the atmosphere what does it. What they call an optical illusion.

MARTINUS: (*Laughs*) It's coming!

GIDEON: What?

MARTINUS: The Day of Judgement. For everybody.

GIDEON: You've been listening to the dominees, haven't you?

MARTINUS: And when that day comes, everybody will stand there and one by one *He* will call our names.

GIDEON: Ja, ja. I know. Time to meet your Maker and all the rest of it. And for the sinners it's down to the old devil and his braaivleis, and for the others it's up to the singing angels for a happy ending. I don't want to spoil it for you, Martinus, but it happens to be fairy stories my friend, stupid fairy stories, and I've heard them all. If you want to believe them, that's your business. I don't. So if you don't mind, keep them to yourself please. This is supposed to be Playland, not Sunday School. I came here to have a little bit of fun, so let's keep it that way. Okay?

7

(*Another laugh from* MARTINUS)

MARTINUS: Ja, that's the way it is. Playland is Happyland! Pretty lights and music. Buy your ticket for the Big Wheel and go round and round and forget all your troubles, all your worries.

That's why they all come. I know. I watch them. Fifteen years I've been with Playland now, and all that time I am watching the people. Noupoort, Cradock, Hanover, Beaufort West, Laingsburg, Colesberg, Middelburg . . . all the places here in the Great Karoo. They pray for rain but they wait for Playland and the happiness machines. And when we switch on the lights and the music, they come. Like moths they come out of the night – the old uncles with the fat aunties, the young boys and the pretty girls, even the little children. They all come to play because they all want to forget.

But it's no good. You can try to forget as hard as you like but it won't help, because all the things you did are written down in the Big Book, and when the day comes you will stand there and *He* will read them to you. And then what you got to say?

GIDEON: Plenty, my friend.

MARTINUS: Ja?

GIDEON: Oh ja! To start with, the so-called 'Big Book'. Just stop now for a moment and try to imagine just how big that book has got to be if what everybody is doing wrong down here is written in it. Ja. You ever thought about that? There's a lot of people in this world, Mr Martinus Zoeloe, and a hell of a lot of 'doing wrong' going on all the time. And also who the hell is writing it all down? They'll need more than shorthand up there if they want to keep up with what's going on down here, that I can tell you.

(MARTINUS *holds up the five fingers of one hand and the thumb of the other.*)

MARTINUS: (*Unperturbed*) Number Six is the big one.

GIDEON: Number Six what?

MARTINUS: The Ten Commandments. Number Six, 'Thou shalt not kill'. That's the big one. Not even your enemy. Not even the man you hate more than anything in the world. If you steal something you can always give it back. If you tell a lie, you can always still tell the truth. But when you kill a man you take his life and you can't give that back. He's dead, and that's the end of it.

GIDEON: (*Agitated*) So why you telling me all this?

MARTINUS: It's in the Bible.

GIDEON: (*Sharply*) I know it's in the Bible. What I'm asking is why you telling me. You think I'm stupid or something? I learnt all about the commandments in Sunday School thank you very much. So just keep your sermons to yourself, okay? If you want to play dominee go preach to those skollie friends of yours.

And anyway, everybody knows there's times when you got to do it.

MARTINUS: What?

GIDEON: Number Six.

MARTINUS: No.

GIDEON: Yes there is! What about self-defence?

(MARTINUS *shakes his head.*)

Or protecting women and children?

(MARTINUS *shakes his head again.*)

What about Defending Your Country Against Communism?

MARTINUS: (*Doggedly*) Aikona!

GIDEON: (*Beside himself with frustration*) Those are all times when it's all right to do it! Even the bloody dominees say so. I've heard them myself. Sermons up in the Operational Area.

MARTINUS: (*Implacable*) No. The Bible says 'Thou shalt not kill thy neighbour'.

GIDEON: So who the hell is talking about neighbours? I'm talking about criminals and communists! No man, this little discussion of ours is now getting out of hand. (*Restraining himself.*) Listen Martinus, I don't want to start a bad argument between us so let me tell you again, and this is now really for the last time, okay? I am gat-full of the Bible. I don't need another dose of it. Do I make myself clear?

You've now really got it on the brain, haven't you? Don't you ever talk about anything else?

9

MARTINUS: Like what?

GIDEON: Like anything, for God's sake. Rugby. Women. Even bloody politics would be better. Talk ANC if you like – all that one-man-one-vote kak – but just change the record for God's sake!

(*Another drink.*)

Somebody I would have liked you to meet is Ou Tollie – he was the Bushman tracker with our unit. He knew what the score was. Never use to join us for church services – just sit there on one side under a thorn-bush and watch us singing our hymns, saying our prayers, and the dominees sermonizing about Heaven and Hell and all the rest of it. So one day I asked him what he thought about things. You know what he said? 'When we die, we die. The wind blows away our footprints and that is the end of us.' Ou Tollie! Ja, he knew what the score was.

They been up there you know. Right round the earth, to the moon and back . . . they even getting ready now to go to Mars . . . and what's more they also got pictures of everything up there, and guess what, my friend . . . there's no sign of your Heaven and Hell anywhere! Put that in your old Bantu pipe and smoke it. Ja! Science, my friend, science! There's a thing up there called a satellite that is going all the way to the End of the World and it's taking pictures all the time and sending them back and all you can see is outer space . . . miles and miles of bugger all. It's almost as bad as the Karoo up there. So I don't know where you think your angels are flying around, but it's certainly nowhere up in the big blue sky, that I can tell you.

(MARTINUS *listens calmly.*)

And finally my friend, just in case you haven't noticed, I would like to point out that the Fires of Eternal Damnation have now gone out, so where the hell is the party?

(MARTINUS *stares at him blankly.*)

It's quarter past seven man. Nearly twenty past.

MARTINUS: So?

GIDEON: So, where's the lights and music? You told me things get going at seven o'clock.

MARTINUS: That's right.

GIDEON: Well for God's sake I'm telling you it's past seven o'clock. (*He shows his watch.*) Look for yourself if you don't believe me.

(MARTINUS *shrugs his shoulders indifferently.*)

Now what the hell is that supposed to mean?

MARTINUS: Maybe the generators is broken down again. There's lots of trouble with the generators. Last month in Noupoort, two nights the generators broke down.

GIDEON: So what must we do?

MARTINUS: Wait. They will try to fix it.

GIDEON: (*Huge disbelief*) I don't believe it! We get ourselves all nicely dressed up, drive for bloody miles to get here, and now we must just stand around and wait like a lot of bloody sheep while they *try* to fix the generators. How long does it take them?

MARTINUS: Sometimes they fix it quick. Sometimes it takes a long time. Sometimes they can't fix it and must send away for spare parts.

GIDEON: And then?

MARTINUS: Nothing.

GIDEON: Nothing what?

MARTINUS: Then nothing happens tonight. Everybody must go home. Last month in Noupoort . . .

GIDEON: To hell with what happened last month in Noupoort. I'm not remotely interested in Noupoort's troubles. They can drop an atomic bomb on that dump as well as far as I'm concerned.

(*Pause.* MARTINUS *calm,* GIDEON *agitated.*)

No man. This is about as much nonsense as a man can take. What a bloody year. No doubt about it now . . . the worst one of my entire life. With all my willpower I hang on until we get to the last arsehole day of it, then I make a special effort and pull myself together and get out of the house, and where do I land up?

A broken-down Playland! And now you tell me I must just go back home if they can't fix the generator? No, my friend. Oh no! You can maybe sell that bullshit to those railway japies in Noupoort, but nobody is going to buy it over here. We weren't born yesterday. If you want to call yourselves Playland you better prove it tonight, otherwise good old Baas Barney will start the New Year with more than just his generators broken.

(*The PA system suddenly crackles into life with static and feedback whine.*)

BARNEY: (*A voice over the PA system*) Testing, testing, one, two, three, four, testing. Can you hear me, Martinus?

MARTINUS: (*Shouting back*) I can hear you, Baas Barney!

BARNEY: Loud and clear?

MARTINUS: Loud and clear, Baas Barney.

BARNEY: All right, Jackson – switch on.

(*The lights of Playland start flickering and after a few false starts they come on and stay on.*)

MARTINUS: (*A good laugh at* GIDEON) There . . . look! Listen! Pretty lights and music! Go forget your troubles white man. Playland is open and waiting for you.

GIDEON *leaves*.

BARNEY: Hello everybody, hello and hello again. Welcome to
Playland. This is your Master of Ceremonies, your old friend
'Barking Barney' Barkhuizen promising you a sensational, a
spectacular evening of fun and thrills to end the year. We've
got a wonderful programme lined up and to start the ball
rolling, here is a special New Year's Eve offer: Buy nine
tickets for any of the rides and you get one free – and
remember, hang on to your ticket stubs because you could be
the winner of one of our fabulous prizes. There's a draw
every hour on the hour! So what are you waiting for? Let's
rock out the old and roll in the new . . . One, two, three and
away we go . . .!
(*An energetic piece of rock and roll music sets the tone and tempo
of the evening. Playland is now in full swing. From the speakers
at the top of the pole a pastiche of old pop songs, rock and roll and
Boeremusiek. Interspersed with these is* BARNEY's *voice making
announcements about the various sideshows and rides, lucky
ticket numbers, lost children and so on and, continuously, the
squeals and shrieks of laughter and terror from people on the
rides.*)

BARNEY: (*Interrupting a pop song*) Hold everything everybody.
Your attention please. This is a very special announcement.
She is blonde, she is beautiful, she is Marie du Toit and she
is eighteen years old today. So come on everybody . . .
(*Singing*) 'Happy birthday to you . . . ' *and so on.*
(*More pop music.*)
Your attention please. Your attention. Please check your
ticket stubs because if you are the holder of number eight-
zero-four-six, I repeat . . . eight-zero-four-six . . . you have
just won yourself and your partner the famous gut-buster
platter at the Happy Rustler Steakhouse. Come to the
information desk for your voucher. Our next draw will be for
a fashion perm at Maison Capri, so hurry up and buy your
tickets for the Big Wheel, the Whip . . .

(*More pop music.*)

This is the lost property department speaking . . . will the parents of little Willie Liebenberg please come to the caravan next to the Wall of Death . . . the parents of little Willie Liebenberg please . . .

(*More pop music.*)

Your attention please, your attention! This is an emergency announcement. Will anyone with an empty and rumbling stomach please report immediately to the stall next to the Rifle Range. We have a sizzling stack of our famous Karoo burgers and Boere dogs in need of urgent gastromedinomical attention. I repeat, anyone . . .

(*More pop music.*)

GIDEON *is in the middle of all this, trying too hard to have a good time. He tells jokes, tries to sing along with the music, and wisecracks about the PA announcements, creating an image of forced and discordant gaiety.*

Later. The night-watchman's camp. MARTINUS *alone.* GIDEON
*returns. Liquor and desperation give a new, aggressive edge to his
behaviour. He wears a silly paper hat and carries a noise-maker.*

GIDEON: (*Singing*)

> . . . baby don't you know I love you so
> Can't you feel it when we touch
> I will never never let you go
> I love you Oh so much.
> . . . but I don't mean you poephol! (*Hollow laugh.*)

How you doing there, Marty?

MARTINUS: You back.

GIDEON: Ja me. Who else? Your old friend Corporal Gideon le
Roux.

MARTINUS: Corporal?

GIDEON: That's it. Two stripes. But listen, forget about the rank.
Just call me Gid. I been thinking about it you see and what
do you say we must just let bygones be bygones? I want us to
be buddies. Me and you. Gid and Marty. Okay?

MARTINUS: Okay.

GIDEON: (*Holding out his hand*) Put it there. (*They shake.*) So then
tell me, how is things with you, Marty?

MARTINUS: (*Humouring him*) I'm doing all right, Gid.

GIDEON: Then why you looking so sad, man? I'm sitting up there
on top of the big wheel, admiring the view, looking down
and seeing everything and everybody and there, in the
corner, all by his lonely self, I see my buddy, poor old
Marty. Everybody else was having such a good time but you
were just sitting there looking so sad. Cheer up man! It's not
the end of the world yet, just the end of a totally useless
bloody year – and we're nearly there Marty! Two more hours
to go and then it's Happy New Year!

MARTINUS: You having a good time, hey, Gid?

GIDEON: You bet. I'm having myself one hell of a good time. I've
tried everything out there – the Lucky Fishpond, shooting

15

wooden ducks with a pellet gun, ping-pong balls in the
clown's mouth . . . you name it, I've done it. And all the
rides as well. Just between you and me, the Ghost Train is
now really bloody stupid – kids' stuff you know . . . But the
Big Wheel . . .! Three times man. Round and round and up
and down. Whoopee! And you know something, it is just
like you said – I've forgotten all my troubles. How about
that! My sick Ma, my stupid job, the stupid bloody foreman
at my stupid bloody job, my stupid bloody car that I already
know won't start when I want to go home – you've got to give
me a push, okay? – I've forgotten them all! And I'm not
finished. I'm going back for more. I want to go round and
round and up and down until I even forget who the bloody
hell I am! (*Hollow laugh*.) How's that?

MARTINUS: That's very good, Gid. But then why you here?

GIDEON: Why am I here? That's a very good question.

MARTINUS: The Big Wheel is over there. There's nothing for you
here.

GIDEON: Oh yes there is! You! My buddy. You are here so that's
why I am here. First thing you learn up there in the bush.
Don't ever desert a buddy.

MARTINUS: You won't forget your troubles if you sit here with
me.

GIDEON: Hey hey hey! Marty. Why you talking like that man? If
I didn't know you so well I would say you was trying to get
rid of me. You're not trying to do that are you . . . because if
you were, then you hurt my feelings man. Eina! You hurt my
feelings bad! (*Hollow laugh*.)

It's only a joke. Hell Marty, listen, as one buddy to
another let me give you a gentle word of advice. Lighten up a
little bit man. You know, try a little smile or a chuckle now
and then. It can be very heavy going with you sometimes.

Anyway, jokes aside now, if you want to know the truth,
the whole truth and nothing but the truth so help me God, I
came back here because I got something for you. A present.
Ja. I mean it when I say I was thinking about you out there.
You ask the others that were up there on the Border with me
– Ou Charlie, or Stan, or Neelsie – all of them. They'll tell

you Corporal Gideon le Roux was always thinking of his
buddies. Because that is the way I was brought up – to think
about others.

So I've got a wonderful present for you. It's going to make
you very happy. It's better than a hundred rides on the Big
Wheel because it won't just help you forget your troubles,
it's going to get rid of them for you . . . and for keeps, my
buddy. That's a money-back guarantee. You ready for it?
It's a New Year's resolution that I made up specially for you
to deal with all your problems. When midnight comes, you
must stand to attention . . .

(*He gets* MARTINUS *standing to attention, removes his balaclava
and puts his paper hat on* MARTINUS'*s head*)

. . . raise your right hand and say, 'I, Martinus Zoeloe, do
solemnly swear that my New Year's resolution for 1990 is
. . . No More Dominees! No More Sermons from the
Dominees! No More Bible Stories from the Dominees! No
More Bullshit from the Dominees! Hallelujah and Amen!'
(*A big hollow laugh.*)

How's that, Marty? I'm telling you man, that is the answer to
all your problems, because that is where they come from –
those black crows up there in the pulpit taking advantage of
simple-minded people like you. You make that your
resolution tonight and I promise you my friend that in 1990
you will be a happy man.

MARTINUS: Like you.

GIDEON: Ja, like me. Well? I'm waiting, Marty.

(MARTINUS *studies* GIDEON *in silence for a few seconds then
goes up to him and puts the paper hat back on his head. He
retrieves his balaclava and returns to his seat.*)

Is it my imagination, Marty, or do you now not really care
too much for my present? Hey? I know you are not the
excitable sort but even so, can't you try to squeeze out a little
'Thank you, Gid'? Haai Marty, I can see you want to break
my heart tonight. Why my buddy? What have I done? That
heart is full of good feelings for you. Don't hurt it. That's not
the way buddies treat each other.

MARTINUS: You make jokes about your heart, but you must be

careful with it. Because *He* can see into it.

GIDEON: Who? Chris Barnard? (*Laughs*.) Joke Marty! Joke.

MARTINUS: All the secrets you hide away there – the big ones, the bad ones – it's no good because *He* knows them.

GIDEON: Marty . . . I've got a horrible feeling you are starting again.

MARTINUS: He knows them all. Ja! Like a skelm in the night looking for your money under your mattress, *He* comes when you are sleeping and *He* finds them and looks at them.

GIDEON: Ja! There you go again – more bloody dominee talk.

MARTINUS: It's not dominee talk.

GIDEON: Yes it is. I know the sound of dominee talk like I use to know the sound of a good cabbage fart from my Dad.

MARTINUS: *He* told me so himself.

GIDEON: Who?

MARTINUS: *Him*.

GIDEON: Him?

MARTINUS: Ja.

GIDEON: Oh I see. This is now the Big Baas himself we're talking about.

(MARTINUS *nods*.)

He spoke to you.

MARTINUS: Ja.

GIDEON: God.

MARTINUS: God Almighty.

GIDEON: He came around here and had a little chat with you.

MARTINUS: It was in a dream. He talked to me in a dream.

(*For a few seconds* GIDEON *is speechless*.)

GIDEON: (*Defeated*) No. No! That's it. I give up. I surrender. I'm waving the white flag, Marty.

MARTINUS: (*Imperturbable as ever*) I dreamed that I was praying like the dominee said I must. I was kneeling and telling *Him* that I was sorry for what I did and wanted forgiveness. And then I heard Him. 'It's no good, Martinus. I can see into your heart. I can see you are not sorry for what you did.' So I said 'That's true, God. I am not sorry.' And He said 'Then I can't forgive and you must go to Hell. All the people who are not sorry for what they did will go to Hell.'

18

GIDEON: Just like that.

MARTINUS: Ja.

GIDEON: And then you woke up.

MARTINUS: Ja.

GIDEON: And you believed it.

MARTINUS: Ja.

GIDEON: And now you also want me to believe it.

MARTINUS: Ja.

GIDEON: Hell Marty, you're asking for a lot tonight. First it's the Bible stories I must believe and now it's your dreams . . .! (*Beginning to lose patience again.*) What's the matter with you man? You can't believe them like they was real, like they was something that really happened to you. A dream . . . is just a bloody dream. It's what goes on in your head when you are sleeping, when your eyes are closed. Like when you imagine things. Don't you even know the difference between that and what is real? Must I also now explain that to you? (MARTINUS *says nothing.* GIDEON *pursues the subject with morbid persistence.*)

Real is what you can believe because you can touch it, and see it, and smell it . . . with your eyes wide open. Next time you sit there in the bush and have a boskak, have a good look at what you leave there on the ground, because that is what real means. When you can show me Heaven and Hell like I can show you shit, then I'll listen to the dominees and believe all their Bible stories. (*Cane bottle reappears.*)

And let me just also say that for somebody who is so certain he is on his way to Hell, you seem to be taking things very easy, buddy boy. According to your Bible that is a fairly serious state of affairs you know. It's not like going to gaol. When you get down there, you stay down there. There's no such thing as getting time off for good behaviour. It's a one-way ticket my friend. Suffering and agony non-stop. And for ever. But if you got no problems with that, then okay. Good luck to you. (*Takes a swig from his bottle.*)

What did you do, Marty? What's the charge the Big Baas is

19

going to read out of the Big Book when the Big Day comes? Must have been a good one if he's given you a one-way ticket for it. Come on man you can tell me. I know how to keep a secret. We're buddies now, remember. Buddies always share their secrets Marty.

(*Still no response from* MARTINUS. GIDEON *continues in a conspiratorial whisper.*)

It was Number Six wasn't it? The Big One. You killed somebody, hey. That's why the Big Baas is so the hell in with you. (*Elated laughter.*) Ja, I knew it man. I'm telling you, the moment I saw you I smelt it. I said to myself 'Be careful Gid. There's something about that bugger.'

MARTINUS: Go back to Playland, Gid. Go ride the Big Wheel.

GIDEON: (*More laughter. He continues greedily*) Not a damn. I'm having a good time here with you. So come on, man. Spill the beans. What happened? Housebreaking and theft? Armed robbery? No. You don't look like that sort. You're not one of those skollies. Something else . . . wait a bit, wait a bit, I've got it! Your woman. Right? You caught your woman with another man! How's that?

MARTINUS: Leave me alone.

GIDEON: (*Laughter*) Looks like I'm getting hot. Who got it Marty? Your woman? The man? Both of them? (*Still more laughter.*) How did you do it? Knife? Did you get away with it?

MARTINUS: I'm telling you again, leave me alone.

GIDEON: Come now, Marty, don't take it personally. I'm only trying to help. All I want is to help you deal with your problems.

MARTINUS: You got no help for me. So go!

GIDEON: (*Brutally*) No!

MARTINUS: What do you want here?

GIDEON: The fucking truth. That's what I want. You killed somebody. It's written all over you man. Think I'm blind? And I want to know who it was.

MARTINUS: I'm telling you nothing.

GIDEON: Oh yes?

MARTINUS: Yes! Nothing!

20

(*Pause.* GIDEON *backs out of the developing confrontation.*)

GIDEON: Okay, if that's the way you want it. I reckon that's the end of buddies then.

MARTINUS: Yes! So go back to your own people.

GIDEON: What people? That fucking herd of Karoo Zombies out there grazing on candy floss? My people? Shit! Any resemblance between me and them is purely coaccidental. You try to talk to them, exchange a few friendly words and they look at you as if you were a fucking freak or something. Playland! Ja, that's where they belong. Two rand to shoot wooden ducks with a pellet gun. We weren't shooting wooden ducks with pellet guns up there on the Border, my friend. While that crowd of fat arses were having joyrides in Playland we were in Hell. Ja! For your information you don't have to wait for Judgement Day to find out what that word means. Hell is right here and now. I can take you to it. It's called the Operational Area and it's not everlasting bonfires either. It's everlasting mud and piss and shit and sweat and dust. And if you want to see the devil I can show you him as well. He wears a khaki uniform, he's got an AK47 in his hands.

MARTINUS: SWAPO.

GIDEON: Ja, that's his name. And he wasn't shooting at wooden ducks either.

MARTINUS: Did you kill him?

GIDEON: The devil? (*Hollow laugh.*) Ja. I killed him. How else do you think I'm here? That's the only way you stayed alive. The Law of the Jungle! That's what we use to say. Kill or be killed . . . and don't think about it.

MARTINUS: (*Pointing at* GIDEON *and laughing triumphantly*) Number Six! You also. Number Six! I'll see you in Hell, Corporal Gideon le Roux.

GIDEON: (*With all the vulgarity he can muster*) Fuck you!

MARTINUS: (*His laughter cut short*) Hey!

GIDEON: That's right. I'll say it again. Fuck you! You can shove Number Six right up your arse. And don't point your fucking finger at me again. It's rude, my boy.

MARTINUS: Haaikona!

21

GIDEON: Haaikona yourself. I'm telling you to mind your own business, Martinus Zoeloe. The secrets in my heart have got nothing to do with you or anybody else.

MARTINUS: (*Restraining himself*) Okay. I mind my own business. And you also. The secrets in my heart got nothing to do with you. So go. There is nothing for you here. This is my place.

GIDEON: Your place?

MARTINUS: Ja. My place. This is the night-watchman's place. I am the night-watchman. You go somewhere else.

GIDEON: Don't you tell me to go! This is still a free country. You people haven't taken over yet.

(*His bottle is empty. He hurls it away and leaves.*)

Later. GIDEON *is back in the bright lights and loud music of
Playland. He is a dark, brooding presence watching the world with
smouldering resentment. Everybody is getting ready for the arrival of
the New Year.*

BARNEY: (*Attempting an American accent*) Good evening ladies and
gentlemen and welcome to this Karoo Broadcasting
Corporation New Year's Eve Special. I am your KBC host
for the evening – 'Barking Barney' Barkhuizen – speaking to
you live from Cape Karooveral where the space shuttle
Playland is waiting on the launching pad . . . primed and
ready for her blast-off into 1990. According to the
countdown clock there is now only three minutes left before
ignition so get ready folks to wave 1989 goodbye. The
weather forecast continues to be favourable – for the launch
and for romance – starry skies and a balmy breeze. Mission
control informs us that the countdown is proceeding
smoothly so it looks as if we're all set for another successful
launch at the stroke of midnight.

And now there is only two minutes to go. An expectant
hush is settling over the large crowd gathered here to
participate in this historic event. Looking at the closed-
circuit television monitors I can see that all the gastronauts in
Playland are putting away the last of their Karoo burgers and
Boere dogs and are now buckling up and bracing themselves
for the G-forces that are going to spin them off into
Playland's 1990 Orbit of Happiness. One minute to go!
We've still got the green light on all systems. The tension is
unbearable ladies and gentlemen as the countdown clock
ticks its way through the last seconds of 1989. On
everybody's lips, the same whispered prayer, Thank God it's
over. Twenty seconds left as we line up for the final
countdown . . . and here it comes . . .!!

Ten-nine-eight-seven-six-five-four-three-two-one-ZERO!!!
We have a launch! We-have-a-launch! Yes, ladies and

gentlemen, Playland has lifted off into 1990 . . .
(*The New Year arrives with an explosion of sound – voices singing, voices cheering, motor car hooters, sirens, fireworks . . . a cacophony that imperceptibly begins to suggest the sound of battle.* GIDEON'*s contribution is to make as much 'Happy New Year' noise as he can, ending up with the singing of* Auld Lang Syne. *This gets progressively more violent and finally degenerates into a wild, wordless animal sound. When he stops, all is silent. He hears nothing except his breathing and his heart beating.*

GIDEON: Easy Gid . . . you're alive! . . . easy does it . . . you're alive . . . it's over . . . it's all over and you're alive . . .
(*The sounds of Playland fade back in.*)

Later. The night-watchman's camp. MARTINUS *is alone. Midnight has come and gone and all that is left of the celebrations are a few distant and receding sounds of revelry. The last piece of music –* Goodnight Sweetheart – *is playing over the PA system.*

BARNEY: (*Now a tired, off-duty voice*) Okay everybody, that's it. Cash up and bring your ticket rolls and money to the caravan. Give it a few more seconds Jackson and then you can start to switch off. And Martinus, make sure everything is locked up properly tonight. We're too near that damned location for my liking. They've got to give us a better site next time otherwise we're not coming here again. New Year's Eve and we only had half the crowd we had at De Aar last month. This lot should go over there for a few lessons in how to have a good time. *Here*, it was hard going tonight. (*A long and audible yawn.*) Ek is moeg, kêrels. Ek is moeg!
(*A few more seconds and then the music is cut off abruptly and Playland's illuminations start to go out.* GIDEON *returns yet again to* MARTINUS. *He stands silently.* MARTINUS *is getting ready for his night shift – old overcoat and kierie.*)

MARTINUS: It's finished, white man. It's all over for tonight. Time for you to go home now. You heard what the music said, 'Goodnight Sweetheart. It's time to go.' (*He laughs.*) Ja, everybody is sad when the happiness machine stop and the lights go out. But don't worry. You can come again tomorrow. Your Playland is safe. Martinus will watch it for you. Martinus will watch all your toys and tomorrow you can come and play again.

But now it is my time! Now night-watchman Martinus Zoeloe is in charge.

Ja! You want to know about me, white man. Okay. I tell you this. I know how to watch the night and wait for trouble. That is my job. While all the sweethearts are lying in bed with their sweet dreams, that is what I am doing – watching the night and waiting for trouble. I do it well. A long time

25

ago I learnt how to sit with the ghosts and look and listen and
wait – and that time I was waiting for Big trouble, white man
. . . bigger trouble than a few drunk location skollies looking
for mischief. So they can come and try their nonsense. I am
ready for them!

(*He brandishes his kierie in traditional style and then sets out on
his rounds.* GIDEON *blocks his path.*)

GIDEON: Where you going?

MARTINUS: To do my job.

GIDEON: No.

MARTINUS: No what?

GIDEON: You're not going anywhere.

MARTINUS: Why not?

GIDEON: Because I say so, that's why. You stay right where you
are. Don't think you can just switch off the fucking lights
and tell me to go home, because I'm telling you it's not over.

MARTINUS: It is, white man. Look! There's nobody left. I tell
you Playland is finished for tonight.

GIDEON: Fuck Playland! I'm talking about you and me. That's
what it's all about now. You and me. Nice and simple. No
complications. You and me. There's things to settle between
us, and now is the time to do it. Right now . . . right here.

MARTINUS: There is nothing between you and me.

(GIDEON *laughs.*)

What do you want from me, white man? All night you keep
coming back. For what? If you want to make trouble go do it
with your own people.

GIDEON: Fuck them as well. I'm not interested in them. It's you I
want. I want to make some nice trouble with you.

MARTINUS: Why? What did I do to you? Nothing!

GIDEON: (*Another wild laugh*) Nothing?

MARTINUS: Yes! I sit here. I mind my own business and then you
come. You come again and again. I didn't call you. I do
nothing to you.

GIDEON: Nothing, Swapo?

MARTINUS: My name is not Swapo.

GIDEON: It is now. I'm calling you Swapo. If you're not my
buddy, that's who you are.

MARTINUS: My name is Martinus Zoeloe.

GIDEON: Martinus Zoeloe se gat!! Name? What the fuck are you talking about? You haven't got a name. You're just a number. Number one, or number two, number three . . . One day I counted you twenty-seven fucking times. I bury you every night in my sleep. You're driving me mad, Swapo. And you call that nothing?

MARTINUS: (*Disturbed by* GIDEON's *violent ramblings*) Haai, haai! You are mad. I'm not talking to you no more.
(*He makes another determined move to leave.* GIDEON *blocks his path again.*)

GIDEON: I said no.

MARTINUS: Let me go.

GIDEON: No. I told you, you're not going anywhere. I haven't finished with you.

MARTINUS: (*Rising anger*) To hell with you. I've finished with you. Get out of my way.

GIDEON: Make me. Go ahead. Make me.
(*He starts pushing* MARTINUS *back.*)

MARTINUS: Don't do that.

GIDEON: (*Another push*) I'll do any fucking thing I like.

MARTINUS: I warn you, white man.

GIDEON: (*Another push*) About what, black man? Warn me about what? You trying to scare me? Don't flatter yourself. There's fuck-all you can say or do that will scare me. But if you want to try something, go ahead.
(*The two men are on the brink of real physical violence.*)
So what are you waiting for? Come, let's see what you can do.

MARTINUS: (*Breaking away*) No Martinus! Stop!
(*He makes a supreme effort to control himself. He returns and confronts* GIDEON.)
Gideon le Roux! I say your name. Please now, listen to me. I put down my kierie. I tell you nicely, I don't want to make trouble with you. Don't you make trouble with me. Leave me alone. Because if we make trouble for each other tonight, then I know what happens.

GIDEON: Oh yes?

MARTINUS: Yes! I will do it again. S'true's God. I do it again.

GIDEON: What?

MARTINUS: Number Six.

GIDEON: Good old Number Six! So I was right. You did kill somebody.

MARTINUS: I killed a white man.

GIDEON: You bullshitting me? You still trying to scare me?

MARTINUS: Andries Jacobus de Lange, the Deceased. I killed him.

GIDEON: You're telling the truth. (*Laughter*.) How about that! It gets better and better. In fact, it's fucking perfect. (*More laughter out of a violent, dark elation.*) I knew it. I knew it all along. The moment I saw you I knew there was something . . . you know . . . between us – me and you. And there it is. You killed a white man. Now we can get down to real business.

MARTINUS: No! There is nothing between you and me.

GIDEON: (*Laughter*) Oh yes there is.

(*Singing*.)

    I will never, never let you go

    I love you Oh so much!

Who was he? The white man?

(*Nothing from* MARTINUS.)

Listen, Swapo, there's a lot of shit we got to clean up tonight, so you better start talking. What happened?

MARTINUS: My woman, she worked for him. For his wife and children. The housework and the washing.

GIDEON: You see! I knew it! I knew there was a woman in it.

MARTINUS: It was in Port Elizabeth. I had a job in the cement factory there. I was saving money to get married. Thandeka, my woman, was living at the white people's house. On Sundays she comes to visit me in the location. And so it was until one day when she comes to me I see that she is unhappy. I asked her what was wrong but she wouldn't tell me anything. Then another time when she comes she was crying and I asked her again and then she told me. She said the white man was coming all the time to her room in the backyard and trying to get into bed with her. She always said

28

no to him and pushed him out. But then one night he beat her and forced her to get into the bed with him.

GIDEON: And then?

MARTINUS: I killed him.

GIDEON: How? How did you do it?

MARTINUS: A knife.

GIDEON: Ja! You bastards like the knife, don't you?

MARTINUS: I sent my woman away. I waited in her room. When the white man opened the door and came in I had my knife ready and I killed him.

GIDEON: Just like that.

MARTINUS: Just like that.

GIDEON: Did he fight?

MARTINUS: Yes, but he wasn't strong, so I killed him quickly. He's in Hell. He didn't even have time to pray to God.

GIDEON: Number Six!

MARTINUS: Number Six. And I'm *not* sorry. When the judge asked me if I was, I told him. I told him that if I saw that white man tomorrow I would kill him again. So then he sentenced me to death and my woman to fifteen years. He wouldn't believe her when she told him what the white man did to her. He said that we killed him because we wanted to rob the house.

GIDEON: Why didn't they hang you?

MARTINUS: They nearly did. I sat in the death cell six months waiting for the rope. I was ready for it. But when there was just three days to go the white man's wife went to the judge and told him that my woman was telling the truth. She told him that her husband had forced other servants to get into his bed. So then they changed my sentence to fifteen years. They let my woman go free. I never saw her again. That is my story.

GIDEON: Story my arse! It's a fucking joke man. A bad joke. You killed that poor bugger just for that? Just for screwing your woman? (*Laughter*.)

You people are too funny. Listen my friend, if screwing your woman is such a big crime, then you and your brothers are going to have to put your knives into one hell of a lot of white men . . . starting with me! Ja. What's the matter with you? Were you born yesterday? We've all done it. And just like you said, knocked on that door in the backyard, then drag her on to the bed and grind her arse off on the old coir mattress. That's how little white boys learn to do it. On your women!

And you want to know something else, Swapo? They like it from us! Your woman was crying crocodile tears. I bet you anything you like she had a bloody good time there with the baas humping away on top of her.

(MARTINUS *rigid, every muscle tense as he tries to control the impulse to throw himself at* GIDEON.)

Now do you understand what I'm saying? If you want to kill that white man again, now's your chance. He's standing right here in front of you.

(GIDEON *waits.*)

Come on! What you waiting for? Try to make it two. You got nothing to lose, Swapo. You already got your one-way ticket. You can't go to Hell twice.

You think you're big stuff don't you because you killed one white man? That's your score. One! And now you think you can maybe make it two. One . . . two. (*Laughter.*) What a bloody joke! You're an amateur, man. What you did was child's play. I was with the pros and for ten years we were up there on the Border sending your freedom fighting brothers to Hell, and I'm not talking about one or two. We were into double figures, man. One amazing bloody day I did the rounds and counted twenty-seven of them that we'd blown away to Kingdom Come. Ja! Twenty-fucking-seven. Do you have the remotest idea what that means? What it feels like to count twenty-seven dead men? You had to have a strong stomach for it my friend. Those brothers of yours were full of shit, and I don't mean their politics. I mean the real stuff. They started stinking even before the sun had cooked them up a bit, because when that happened, when they'd been in the oven for a couple of days, as we use to say, then I'm telling you, you didn't eat meat for a week.

(*Speaking with manic intensity.*) That was the first thing I

use to do you see. When it was all over – the shooting and
screaming – all that fucking noise like the world was coming
to an end, when suddenly it was quiet like now, I would take
a deep breath, say to myself 'You're alive, Gid', then walk
around and count. I always wanted to know how many there
were, you see. Even before the OC asked for a body count I
was out there doing it. You could take your time you see,
walk around slowly and carefully and do it properly like my
Pa use to do when he counted his cabbages in the backyard.
The Oubaas was crazy about cabbages, man, specially the
way my Ma use to cook it for him, in a pot with nice pieces of
fat mutton. It made him fart like an Impala ready for take-
off, but he had to have his cabbage. So every morning it was
'Come Gideon, let's go count our blessings,' and I would
hold his hand and walk next to him and say nicely after him
'One cabbage, two cabbage, three cabbage . . .' that's how I
learnt to count. Even before I was in school man I knew how
to count my blessings. But now it wasn't cabbages any more,
it was 'One Swapo, two Swapo, three Swapo . . .' My very
first time I counted there was eight of them. Shit man, that
was something new for me. The only dead person I had ever
seen was my Pa when we all said goodbye to him in his coffin
and now suddenly there I was counting eight of them – lying
all over the place, some of them with pieces missing. Then
for a long time it looked as if fifteen was going to be the
record until that follow-up when we ambushed a whole
bloody unit . . . and when it came time to count . . .!
Twenty-fucking-seven of them! I couldn't believe it man. A
new record! 'Twenty-seven Swapo cabbages in the garden,
Sir!'

(*He salutes.* MARTINUS *just stares at him.*)

So where's your sense of humour? That's a joke. Didn't you
get it? Swapo cabbages. I counted the dead men like my Pa
use to count his fucking cabbages. So don't just stand there
and stare at me like a bloody baboon. Laugh!

MARTINUS: No.

GIDEON: (*Rage*) What do you mean 'No'? It's a bloody good joke
man. 'Twenty-seven Swapo cabbages in the garden, Sir!'

MARTINUS: Then why don't you laugh?

GIDEON: You want to hear laughter? I'll give you fucking laughter.

(*He makes a violent and grotesque attempt at laughter that spirals away into the sound of his pain and torment. He is left totally defeated.*)

MARTINUS: (*After a pause*) No, you are not laughing. (*He speaks quietly, calmly.*) What is the matter with you white man? What is it you are doing tonight? You come here to me, but I don't want you. I tell you so, but you come back. You come back again and again. You make bad trouble between us. You try to make me kill you and now you tell me you are laughing at dead men but I can see it is a lie. Why? Why are you telling me that lie? Why are you trying so hard to make me believe it?

(GIDEON *denies nothing*)

I remember once when I also tried very hard to tell a lie. It was when I was still small. I broke the window in our house in the location. I was very frightened because my father was a very cross man. So when he came home from work I told him that the other boys playing in the street had done it. I tried very hard to make him believe it. It was no good. He could see my lie and so I got the hiding. When it was finished and I had stopped crying, he said to me, 'That was for breaking the window. Now you get another one, a good one, for telling me a lie and trying to hide what really happened.' Is that why you are doing it? Are you hiding something away like little Martinus?

(*Disturbed by the direction his thoughts are taking.*) Aikona! Aikona Martinus! Suka! Leave it now. Go to work. Leave him. His nonsense is not your business.

(*He tries to leave.*)

Fuck you, white man! I'll see you in Hell. Hey! I said fuck you, white man!

(*No reaction from* GIDEON. MARTINUS *returns.*)

Okay. I am going to ask you, but you must tell me no more lies. What is the true feeling inside you?

GIDEON: Leave me alone.

MARTINUS: No, you must tell me now. You must speak the
truth. What is the feeling you got inside you?

GIDEON: Feeling? I've got fucking feelings for Africa, man.
Which ones do you want? Bad feelings, sick feelings, hate
feelings?

MARTINUS: Inside you now. Your feelings about what you did.
The dead men. Twenty-seven dead men.

GIDEON: No! Leave me alone. I say fuck you to you as well. Go
do your work. Go do anything you like – just go. You're
right, there's nothing between you and me.

(*Pause.* MARTINUS *decides. He sits.*)

MARTINUS: Listen to me now. I am going to tell you something
else. When I was sitting in the death cell, waiting, the prison
dominee came to visit me. Dominee Badenhorst. He came to
me every day with his Bible. He read to me about the
Commandments – specially Number Six – Thou Shall Not
Kill. He said to me, 'Martinus, you have sinned. You have
killed a man. But if you pray and ask God for Forgiveness
and he looks into your heart and sees that you are really
sorry, then he will forgive you.'

Then I said to him, 'But I am not sorry.' Then he said,
'Then you will go to Hell, Martinus.'

'I can't help it, Dominee,' I said, 'then I will go to Hell,
but I can't feel sorry.'

He wouldn't believe me. 'No,' he said, 'that is not so. You
are a good man, Martinus. Look deep into your heart. I
know you are sorry for what you did.'

'Listen Dominee,' I said, 'I say it to the Judge and now I
say it to you also – if I saw that white man tomorrow, I would
kill him again. It would make me very very happy to kill him
again.'

The dominee was very sad and prayed for me. There in the
cell, on his knees, he prayed to God to make me feel sorry.
But it is no good. I still don't have that feeling. All the years I
was in gaol, and all the years I sit here by the fire, I ask
myself, 'What is it that makes a man feel sorry? Why doesn't
it happen inside me?' Baas Joppie – he was the prison
carpenter, I was his handlanger – he was sorry. He killed his

33

father and he was so sorry for doing it he cried all the times he told me about it. And Jackson Xaba – they hanged him – guilty four times for rape and murder, he told me also he was sorry. But me . . .?

(*He shakes his head.*) The dominee said that if I looked deep into my heart I would find that feeling. I try. I look inside. When I sit here every night I look inside and I find feelings, strong feelings for other things. When I remember Thandeka and I wonder where she is, I feel a big sadness inside me. Or when I just sit by the fire when it is cold and the tea is hot, that makes me feel good inside. Bread and meat, good! Rain! Rain falling in this dry Karoo – very good! I even find feelings for dead dogs. But for him – Andries Jacobus de Lange, the Deceased, the man I killed – *No*!

And now there is you.

(*Again shaking his head in disbelief.*) You have got that sorry feeling for what you did, for the men you killed, haven't you?

(GIDEON *tries to wave him away.*)

When did it come? When you killed them? Later? When you counted them?

GIDEON: What difference does it make when it happened? It happened!

(*A voice shorn of all deception.*) I was too revved up at the time to feel anything. When you're in the middle of something like that and you've got your finger on the trigger of that R3, there's only one thought in your head: You're alive, Gid! Keep it that way, man. Stay fucking alive. The only thing going on inside you is a sort of wild feeling, but I mean like really wild man. And anyway because it was a follow-up we didn't even rest, so there wasn't time to think about anything. We just kept on going after them.

We came back that way a few days later. Hell, man, it was terrible. A man starts smelling bad the minute he's dead, but when he's been lying out in the sun for a few days . . .! Believe me I wasn't exaggerating when I said you can't eat your food afterwards. Me and another chap was detailed to take the bodies and dump them in a big hole. Oh boy! First

we had to load them on to the back of the lorry, one by one –
we had to wear gloves and masks it was so bad – then we
drove over to the hole. When we got there I see this old
woman come out of the bush and stand there and watch us.
She didn't do anything or say anything – she just stood there
watching.

So we back the lorry up to the hole and started . . . He
grabs the hand, I grab a leg, drag it to the edge and then . . .
into the hole. First you kind of try to do it nicely you know,
because after all they was human beings, but by the time you
get half way through you just don't give a damn any more –
it's hot and you're feeling naar so you just chuck them in. All
the time I was doing this I had a strange feeling that it
reminded me of something, but I couldn't remember what it
was. And the old woman was still standing there watching
us. I couldn't take it any more so I started shouting and
swearing at her, telling her to go away, and while I was doing
that suddenly it came to me, the thing I was trying to
remember.

It was the time we was on holiday at Mossel Bay – me and
my Mom and my Dad. I was still just a little outjie in a khaki
broek. Every day me and my Dad would take his fishing rod
and go down to the rocks. He would put on some bait and
throw out and then wait for a big one. My job was to catch
him the small fishes in the rock pools for him to use as bait.
So one day I catch this lekker fat little fish and I'm all excited
and I start to cut it up and then – *Here*! man, hundreds of
little babies jump out of its stomach on to the rock. Just so
big . . . (*indicating with his fingers*) . . . little babies man! –
they already has little black dots where their eyes was going
to be – jumping around there on the rock. And the mother
fish also, with her stomach hanging open where I had cut
her, wagging her tail there on the rock. And I looked down at
all of this and I knew man, I just knew that what I had done
was a terrible sin. Any way you look at it, whether you
believe all that stuff about Heaven and Hell and God
Almighty or not it makes no difference. What I had done was
a sin. You can't do that to a mother and her babies. I don't

35

care what it is, a fish or a dog or another person, it's wrong!

So then what the hell was going on man? There I was on the back of that lorry doing it again, only this time it was men I was sommer throwing into that hole. Maybe one of them was that woman's son. Maybe I had killed him. That did it. Something just went inside me and it was snot and tears into that face mask like I never cried in my whole life, not even when I was small. I tore off the mask and gloves and got off the lorry and went over to where the old woman had been standing, but she was gone. I ran into the bush to try and find her, I looked and called, but she was gone. That's where they found me the next day. They said I was just walking around in a dwaal.

MARTINUS: What did you want with the old woman?

GIDEON: I wanted to tell her about that little boy. I wanted to tell her that he knew what was right and wrong. I don't know what happened to him, what went wrong in his life, but he didn't want to grow up to be a man throwing other men into a hole like rotten cabbages. He didn't want to be me. And when I had told her all that, I was going to ask her for forgiveness . . . but she was gone.

(*A silence between the two men.* MARTINUS *finally understands.*)

MARTINUS: So that is it. That is why you keep coming back tonight. Forgiveness.

GIDEON: Ja.

MARTINUS: For twenty-seven dead men.

GIDEON: Ja.

MARTINUS: How many did you kill?

GIDEON: Doesn't make any difference, man. You killed one, you killed them all.

MARTINUS: Number Six twenty-seven times! And you say there was also other times?

GIDEON: Ja.

MARTINUS: No! That's too big for me, white man. I'm just a night-watchman. Go ask God for that forgiveness.

GIDEON: Forget about Him, man. He's forgotten about us. It's me and you tonight. The whole world is me and you. Here! Now! (*Anger and bitterness.*) Do you think I wanted it to be this

36

way? Do you think that if I could have chosen the other person in my world tonight it would be you? No such luck. We've got no choices, man. I've got you and you've got me. Finish and klaar. Forgive me or kill me. That's the only choice you've got.

MARTINUS: If I forgive you, then I must forgive Andries Jacobus de Lange, and if I forgive him, then I must ask God to forgive me . . . and then what is left? Nothing! I sit here with nothing . . . tonight . . . tomorrow . . . all my days and all my nights . . . nothing!

(*Violent rejection.*) No! It's too late to talk forgiveness to me. It's like you say, it's all finish and klaar now. We've done what we've done. Number Six – you and me. So leave it alone. We go to Hell and that is the end of it.

(*Pause. It is Martinus's moment of defeat.*)

Haai white man! Why did you bring me so much trouble tonight? Forgive you or kill you! What do I know about forgiveness? Nothing. My heart knows how to hate Andries Jacobus de Lange. That is all it can do. But kill you? No. I don't know if I can do it again.

I know I have only killed one man, but I have done it too many many times. Every night when I sit here I wait again in that little room in the backyard. I wait again in the dark with my knife, I wait for him and when he comes I kill him – again and again – too many times.

GIDEON: Ja. I know what you're saying. It burns you out, hey? Kill somebody and sooner or later you end up like one of those landmine wrecks on the side of the road up there on the Border – burnt-out and bloody useless.

So where the hell did it go wrong, man? Because it wasn't meant to be like this. Isn't that so? I mean, did you want to spend your whole life like you just said – hating one man and spooking with him every night in that little room where you killed him?

MARTINUS: No. I wanted to do other things with my life.

GIDEON: I didn't want to spend mine hating myself. But look at me. That's all I do now. Everything else is just pretending. I try to make it look as if I'm getting on with things like everybody else: I wake up, go to work, joke with the other ous, argue with the foreman, go home, eat supper, watch TV with my Ma . . . but it's all a lie man. Inside me I'm still at that hole outside Oshakati. That's where I go every bloody night in my dreams – looking for that old woman in the bush . . . and never finding her.

(*Parodying himself.*) 'You're alive, Gid!' What a bloody joke. I'm as dead as the men I buried and I'm also spooking the place where I did it.

(*Pause. First light of the new day.*)

It's getting light. Hell, have we been talking that long?

MARTINUS: Ja, we've been talking long.

GIDEON: I can see you now. Yessus, you're an ugly bugger.

MARTINUS: You too.

GIDEON: This is about the time when me and my Dad use to wake up, get dressed and then go open the hok and let them out – even in winter – early morning, just before sunrise. Then we would go back into the kitchen and make our coffee and take it out into the backyard and watch them flying around. Sometimes they was up there in the sunlight, while we were still in the shadows! It always made us laugh. I don't know why, but we would just stand there, drink our coffee, watch the dawn manoeuvres of the Karoo Squadron . . . and laugh our bloody heads off. And there were no lies in that laugh. It was for real. That was how we felt inside.
So . . .

(MARTINUS *is silent.*)

That's it then. New Day. New Year. Did I wish you Happy New Year last night?

MARTINUS: No.

GIDEON: Well better late than never as they say. Happy New Year to you and . . . what else? . . . Ja, thanks for the chat.

(*An awkward, hesitant moment between the two men.* GIDEON *starts to leave.*)

MARTINUS: (*Impulsively and with conviction.*) To hell with it! I have got something to say.

GIDEON: What?

MARTINUS: I also want to see them. Those pigeon-birds. Flying

38

round up there like you say. I also want to see that.

GIDEON: What are you saying, man?

MARTINUS: I am saying to you that when Playland comes back here next time – Christmas and New Year – I want to do it like you said . . . look up in the sky, watch the pigeon-birds flying and drink my tea and laugh!

GIDEON: Do you mean that?

MARTINUS: I am saying it to you because I mean it. To hell with spooking! You are alive. So go home and do it. Get some planks, find some nails and a hammer and fix that hok. Start again with the pigeon-birds.

(*Pause*.)

Do you hear what I am saying, Gideon le Roux?

GIDEON: I hear you, Martinus Zoeloe.

MARTINUS: Do you understand what I am saying?

GIDEON: Ja, I think so. And you also hey. Get out of that little room, man. Let old Andries spook there by himself tonight. Do you understand me, Martinus Zoeloe?

MARTINUS: Ja, I understand you.

GIDEON: Good. And to prove that you are alive and not a spook come give me a push, man. I know that bloody tjorrie of mine is not going to start again. Been giving me trouble all bloody week. I don't know what is wrong with it. Been into the garage two times already this month . . .

(*They walk off together*.)

END

THE ARTS AND SOCIETY

Edited extracts from a talk delivered at Rhodes University in 1991
in which Fugard explores the relationship between the two.

There are as many ways and reasons for writing a play as there are
individual playwrights. All I can talk about with any authority is
my own personal experience. Just of late there has been an
attempt on the part of certain political groupings in the country to
tell artists what they should be doing, what their social obligations
are, and how they should go about discharging them. I believe
very strongly that artists should be left to look after themselves in
this regard. When it comes to the arts, nobody has the right to
make rules for another.

So let me start off by saying this: I am more in love with my
craft as a playwright – more passionately committed to theatre
and excited by its extraordinary power, its extraordinary
imaginative freedom, than I have ever been and I think one of the
main reasons for this is the powerful dynamic that exists in South
African theatre.

Talking to audiences overseas, particularly in America, I have
claimed for South Africa an almost unique dynamic in terms of
the relationship between the event on the stage and the political
and social reality out in the streets. I personally cannot think of
another country where there is as direct and electrifying a
relationship between the two, where the drama on the streets is
being so immediately reflected by the drama on the stage.

Not even in Eastern Europe where even more dramatic political
change has taken place is theatre as directly in touch with the
events out on the streets as is the case in our country.

This dynamic, which was virtually non-existent when I did my
first plays in Johannesburg thirty-five years ago is, I repeat, one of
the main reasons for the depth and strength of my commitment to
the medium.

One small point in parenthesis. Don't let what I have just said
leave you with the impression that now, on the brink of my

41

sixtieth birthday, I pick up my pen and sail with confidence into the writing of a new play.

I am in fact at work on a new play at the moment* and I still find myself terribly intimidated by the reality of blank paper. None of my past experience in writing plays helps me deal with what I describe as the 'inquisition of blank paper' when I face up to it at the outset of a new work.

Now in spite of all I have said about the exciting, committed energy of our theatre, I must also tell you that I find myself very frustrated by the label 'political playwright' which I have ended up with.

I can understand how it happened. There is a very obvious political spin-off to the plays I write. But then my work is not unique in that regard. I don't think it is possible to tell a South African story accurately and truthfully and for it *not* to have a political spin-off.

I believe we live in one of the most highly politicised societies in the world. In other countries people take their politics seriously enough, but they don't talk, argue, dream, live it, to the extent we do. The South African reality is surely unique in that regard.

When I take stock of an ordinary day in my life, I can't find any area of my living which politics has not invaded; I can't find any area of experience in which the political issues, the political realities do not, in some way or another, have a resonance. They are there in the most intimate relationships I have with other human beings, and most pertinently of course in the relationship I have with myself.

Nevertheless, even though I can understand how I have ended up with that label I still find it very frustrating because I think it creates an expectation that gets in the way of people receiving the play I have written. Even more seriously, I think, in the way that it tries to take away certain freedoms from me as a writer.

If people are sitting in an audience for one of my plays waiting for a political message, they are going to be very disappointed. I am a storyteller, not a political pamphleteer, and because of their misguided anticipation they will, in all likelihood, not get the story I am trying to tell.

* The play referred to is *Playland*.

This has happened with some frequency in my career, particularly on the part of the critics who, quite frankly, are too often the laziest members of the audience. They are the ones who came up with the label in the first place. They keep me pigeonholed because it solves a lot of problems for them. Pigeonholing a writer gives you the comfortable illusion that you know who and what he or she is.

You see, the only way to stay alive creatively as a writer is to constantly generate for yourself new challenges, to try to break out of the mould of old habits and formulae, turn corners and go in new directions. I am very conscious of this because I have felt the need for it at several critical periods in my writing life.

I have seen a few fellow playwrights of my time die creatively because they were incapable of generating new challenges for themselves. You undergo profound emotional and intellectual changes as an individual in the living of your life, and your writing has to keep up with this. If it doesn't, you will end up 'imitating' yourself, or worse than that, imitating a self that no longer exists. What was at first a deeply felt personal truth becomes a hollow formula, repeated now simply to stay in the good books of the critics who liked it when it first appeared. I could not go back at this point and write a play like *The Blood Knot*, the play in which I discovered my voice for the first time.

A very changed Athol Fugard is writing the new play, yet so many critical definitions of my work are still the old ones generated by *The Blood Knot*.

A personal example of what I am talking about came with my play *A Place with the Pigs*, which I *know* is a very good play, possibly one of my best, and will one day confound the critics who did not think so. But it was seemingly not about South African politics and that was enormously disconcerting both to the critics and to the audiences. A play about a Russian soldier who deserted the front line and hid in a pigsty for thirty-seven years? What has happened to Fugard? I acted in the première productions in the United States and South Africa and I could literally hear the audience scratching its head and asking, 'When is he going to start talking about what we expect him to talk about?'

That is a very severe limitation when you're a writer. It's a

43

particularly severe limitation in theatre because theatre is a very immediate medium. Judgements are passed very quickly, too quickly, in my opinion . . . and the success or failure of a play that has taken nine months to write is decided overnight. It's not like a novel which can lie around and be taken up and reassessed and brooded on and thought about. The notices are out there the next day and regrettably South African audiences are now also allowing the critics to do all their thinking for them.

I said earlier that I think of myself as a storyteller, that I don't preach political sermons. In all the writing that lies behind me not once has an idea been the provocation that led to the writing of a new play. The genesis of a new work has always been something that I have experienced personally, or something that I have seen happen to other people as I have gone about the business of living my life, or even something that I've read in a newspaper. Somehow or other there have always been the faces of people involved, the realities of actual lived lives.

Obviously there is an intellectual content to a good story as well. Ideally you should leave the theatre with both head and heart excited. What I am talking about is the *genesis* of new work on my side and for me that has always been an image of a particular individual or a group of individuals, something that they had done or something that was done to them.

And what is more, they are usually desperate individuals – human desperation is the real substance of theatre. Nobody has ever written a good play about a group of happy people who started off happy and who were happy all the way through. Whether it's *Antigone* or *Mother Courage* or some of those extraordinary disembodied voices which come out of Samuel Beckett's universe, we are talking about human desperation – that is the substance of drama – and in South Africa if you have found a desperate individual, nine times out of ten you have also found a desperate political situation.

I end up writing a play when that external event, that thing I read in the newspaper, that incident I saw on the street or that little thing that happened to me, coincides with what I can only describe as a build-up of subconscious pressure within myself to the point where it needs release.

When I look back on my writing life I am conscious of how leading up to the writing of every new play there has been – without my necessarily being aware of it at first – the build-up of a certain kind of psychic pressure inside me which has intensified with time and which finally becomes so acute that I need a story into which I can release it.

The Swedish poet Tranströmer has a line to the effect that when the external event coincides with the internal reality the poem happens. That is how it works for me as a playwright.

What I have also discovered is that it doesn't work if I try to use something that is immediately around me, some image from the day that I've just lived or from a day past or from a month past – somehow it only works when the image is one that has lain around in my life gestating for a long time, more often than not for years. The seminal images of my new play go back all of twenty-five years in my notebooks.

I am an addicted keeper of notebooks. When I see things which I think might be useful to me in the future they go into my notebook and that is where I always look when I realize that I am pregnant again.

I am not always aware of the nature of the pressure that has built up in me and what is really involved when I suddenly take up an image and develop it into a play. Awareness of what was actually going on in my subconscious usually only comes some time after the event.

A good example of all of this is my play *The Road to Mecca*. About seven or eight years ago, having known about her for at least fifteen years, I suddenly found myself thinking about a play based on the life and work of Helen Martins of Nieu-Bethesda. What I realize now is that my hidden agenda in writing that play was an attempt to understand the genesis, nature and consequences of a creative energy.

One of the great fears of my life has been the possible drying up of my creative energy. What would I do if I ever found that I could not write again and there was still a lot of time left to live?

I once said in an interview that the only truly safe place I have ever known in this world, in this life that I have lived, was at the centre of a story as its teller. I speak to you with a measure of authority and confidence tonight only because when I go back to Port Elizabeth I go back to my desk where I am writing a new play and because of that I know who I am, what I am, where I am and why I'm there. All the whys, whos, whats and wheres of my life are taken care of when I am writing.

I go through a terrible kind of limbo existence between one act of storytelling and another. I have only once experienced that indescribable hell called writer's block when you just can't get it down on paper, and although it was many years ago, that once was enough. It is a form of anguish that still frightens me when I think about it now. Dealing with that fear was, I now believe, one of the main reasons for writing *The Road to Mecca*.

It is not a biographical play about the real Helen Martins. The Miss Helen of my *The Road to Mecca* is actually a self-portrait. It was only after I had written the play that I realized what I had been trying to do. I used the symbolic vocabulary of the play to understand my own personally dreaded moment of darkness – the extinction of my creativity.

What happens when all the candles go out? What Miss Helen realizes of course is that to be a true master you have got to know not only how to light them, but also how to blow them out. This recognition has, I think, been the inspiration behind some of the most moving works of art. When you listen to Strauss's four last songs or Mahler's *Das Lied von der Erde* you are in fact in the presence of artists who have recognized the need for renunciation. The affirmation in my play is Miss Helen's recognition and acceptance of that necessity.